Publishing Credits

Dona Herweck Rice, *Editor-in-Chief*
Lee Aucoin, *Creative Director*
Kristy Stark, M.A.Ed., *Senior Editor*
Torrey Maloof, *Editor*
Kristine Magnien, M.S.Ed., *Associate Education Editor*
Neri Garcia, *Senior Designer*
Stephanie Reid, *Photo Researcher*
Rachelle Cracchiolo, M.S.Ed., *Publisher*

Image Credits

cover: Thinkstock; pp. 3,4, 8, 13, 16, 19, 21, 25, 26, 31, 32, 34, 36, 40 iStockphoto; all other images from Shutterstock.

Teacher Created Materials

5301 Oceanus Drive
Huntington Beach, CA 92649-1030
http://www.tcmpub.com
ISBN 978-1-4333-5272-0
© 2013 Teacher Created Materials, Inc.

MW00979935

Contents

Dear Family,

Your eighth grader is beginning another important year of transition. In most school systems, this is the last year before high school, with all the responsibilities and challenges that period brings. Your teen's changes in the brain and physical development that began a few years ago may be slowing down—or may still be in play. And it's likely that your teen has had some encounters with peer pressure.

Your role this year, besides being patient and keeping your sense of humor (and remembering what it was like to be a newly minted teen), will be to serve as your teen's coach as much as anything! He or she will need gentle but firm guidance while navigating the increasing demands of school and life outside school. Keeping the lines of communication open continues to be critical so that you can influence your teen's decision-making process.

Take time to learn how your teen's teachers communicate so that you know what is happening in school. Newsletters and postings on a website can help you keep ahead of the game. You have a busy year ahead, and it may include that first dance or major graduation. We hope this parent guide gives you some useful tips for ensuring that it's a successful year!

One last thought...

Remember when you thought your parents didn't know anything? You probably made your share of mistakes, and now, here you are, trying to be a great parent. Good luck...and have some fun, too!

A Call
to Order

If you have a messy teen, you'll want to compromise so that lost materials don't complicate getting through the school week. Deciding together how this will be accomplished improves the chances of the plan being implemented.

Try some of these ideas to help establish good habits.

In- and Out-Boxes

Organization can be as simple as baskets or bins designated for schoolbooks, backpack, sports equipment—or in-boxes and out-boxes that everyone uses in a central location.

Sticky Notes

Narrow the field by having a daily posting of key events in a prominent place, such as on the refrigerator. Review it before everyone leaves for the day. Use sticky notes for last-minute changes or updates.

Planning System

Begin the year by establishing planning systems for everyone. Use the school calendar to enter the upcoming events, and add routine items, such as lessons and sports practices. Let your teen manage the day-to-day entries, but take time to review everyone's schedules at least once a week.

Cleaning Schedule

Keep ahead of the clutter by having a regular time when everyone is responsible for cleaning or organizing.

SPRING
CLEANING CHECKLIST:

- ☑ CLEAN WINDOWS
- ☐ GARDENING
- ☐ DUSTING
- ☐
- ☐
- ☐

One last thought...

Be a good model for organizing your life, but don't get frustrated if your teen isn't interested.

Avoiding
Homework Hassles

Help your student navigate middle school by keeping in touch with the staff through the school website and/or newsletters and conferences.

Consider these tips to help with homework.

Keep in Touch

Some teachers work hard to make communication easy, using a call-in phone number or dedicated portion of the website for homework assignments.

Slow Down

Take the time to lend a helping hand, if only to keep your teen on track.

Work Space

It may be really difficult for your teen to move from desk to desk at school and then be expected to work at a desk at home. Create a space nearby where you can be available in case your eighth grader needs additional help.

Praise

Your teen may act like it's no big deal, but sincere praise is appreciated at any age: "You've really thought this through." "This is going to be a great report." "This effort should impress any teacher."

One last thought...

A computer is great for conducting research and finding examples of math solutions. Be sure to monitor the websites your eighth grader visits, both for accuracy of content and being age-appropriate.

Find Time
to Talk

With cell phones, text messages, and email, there is an increasing amount of written and verbal shorthand. Your teen may have little to say to you, but he or she may eat up hours of cell phone time with friends.

These ideas might help you
sneak in time for talk.

Meaningful Conversations

Be alert to opportunities to have thoughtful conversations by being an attentive, open-minded listener.

Daily Discussion

Incorporate a daily discussion of the news or community events into your day. Have members of the family read aloud the advice column or a favorite cartoon of the day.

Family Meeting

Maintain a regular time for a short weekly family meeting. Let each family member bring up an issue, if necessary.

Join 'Em

No reason why you can't text your teen! Communicate anything from schedule updates to encouragements.

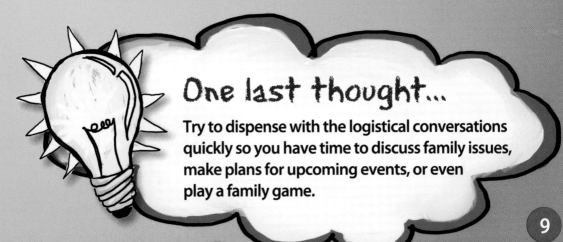

One last thought...

Try to dispense with the logistical conversations quickly so you have time to discuss family issues, make plans for upcoming events, or even play a family game.

Your Sleepyhead

Your teen won't believe that sleep is important—until the weekend! Research shows that teens can't help wanting to stay up late and get up late. Your teen needs about nine hours of sleep—and one hour of that shouldn't be during first period.

Here's what can happen to a sleep-deprived teen:

- Concentration problems
- Problem-solving difficulties
- Memory problems
- Anger, sadness, or depression
- Susceptibility to illness
- Eating disorders

Make the bedroom comfortable for sleeping (e.g., temperature, light, noise level).

Establish a routine that includes a relaxing shower or bath just before bedtime.

Avoid sugar, caffeine, stimulating music, television, computer games, and videos before bedtime.

Get the next day's clothes and backpack ready.

Use a notepad by the bed to write down last-minute to-dos. This reduces stress.

Take a short "power nap" in the afternoon if you're really tired. Don't nap close to bedtime.

Avoid sleeping late on the weekends. It can affect the quality of sleep during the week.

One last thought...

Some teens do have sleep disorders, such as restless legs syndrome. If your teen has persistent problems, have him or her keep a sleep diary. If adopting the practices above don't help, see a doctor.

Break
It Down

The best students work toward their goal every day. Preparation is the key to success. Help your teen learn test-taking skills and strategies so that he or she is better prepared.

• •

These tips should help your student with homework and tests.

Before the Test

- Use a study guide, or work the sample problems.

- Identify your weak areas. Extra problems can usually be found in the back of a textbook or on the Internet.

- Read tough problems aloud more than once.

- Work with a partner.

- Restate tricky problems.

- Turn a word problem into an equation, a sketch, or a chart. Substitute simpler numbers.

- Look for patterns and shortcuts.

- Check your answer by working a problem backwards.

- Take breaks.

During the Test

- Read the directions carefully. If you don't understand them, whisper them.

- Scan the test and complete the easiest problems first.

- Use trial and error (guess it and check it).

- Is it multiple choice? Work a problem backward using the most likely answer.

- Estimate. If an answer seems illogical, it probably is.

- Monitor your time, and pace yourself.

- Review your work if time permits.

One last thought...

Have your eighth grader make up tests for you to take. The process of making a test—and analyzing *your* mistakes—will help him or her get into the head of a test maker.

Top 10

Things Your Eighth Grader
Needs to Know

1. **Theme or central idea** of a text and how to analyze its development

2. **Meanings of words and phrases** as they are used in a text, including figurative and connotative meanings

3. **Informative, explanatory, narrative, and short** research projects

4. Radicals and integer **exponents**

5. **Proportional relationships**, lines, and linear equations

6. **Defining, evaluating, and comparing functions;** using functions to model relationships between quantities

7. **Motion, forces, and structure** of matter

8. Developing their own questions and **performing investigations**

9. Major events preceding the founding of the nation and its significance to the **development of America**

10. **Events from the Constitution up to World War I,** with an emphasis on America's role in the war

Read
On!

If you need to get your teen talking, read some books together. If there is a tough topic you need to tackle, check with your librarian. A good young-adult novel might be the way to open the door to conversation.

Help your teen with these reading tips.

Shared Reading

If your child is struggling with a book, get your own copy and do a shared reading: Take turns reading chapters aloud, discussing the vocabulary and plot. Light reading can help balance out a tough day.

Community Reads

Community reads, during which everyone reads and discusses the same novel, have sprung up in many towns.

Family Reads

Try a family read, giving members a chance to choose the book. If you have a younger family member, choose a book appropriate for reading aloud.

Reading and Writing

Have your teen take notes, create questions, or note difficult words as you read aloud. Discuss the notes, and then reverse roles.

Reader's Theater

Find reader's theater scripts at the library or on the Internet and read the scripts as a family. If you have a budding writer, have him or her turn a novel into a script for the family to read.

One last thought...

If your teen occasionally doesn't have homework, establish that homework time will be used for reading. If your teen is a reluctant reader, have word puzzles, magazines, and graphic novels (similar to comic books) on hand.

Teen
Reads

Not just for teens, these young adult books are sure to make you a fan. Try some! Find other books by authors you and your teen enjoy.

• •

Here are some books you should find.

- *The Absolute True Diary of a Part-Time Indian* by Sherman Alexie

- *The Hunger Games* by Suzanne Collins

- *Anne Frank: The Diary of a Young Girl* by Anne Frank

- *The Outsiders* by S.E. Hinton

- *The Giver* by Lois Lowry

- *The Angel Experiment* by James Patterson

- *Where the Red Fern Grows* by Wilson Rawls

- *The Help* by Kathryn Stockett

- *Roll of Thunder, Hear My Cry* by Mildred D. Taylor

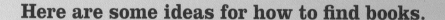

Here are some ideas for how to find books.

- Library book sales
- Garage sales
- Sales at bookstores
- Book swap with neighbors

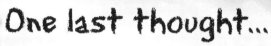

One last thought...

After reading young-adult literature, read more books written by authors you and your teen both enjoy!

Write Now!

Familiarize yourself with some of these writing projects so that you can help prepare your teen, especially since he or she may be facing a state writing exam during this school year.

• •

Expository or Informational Writing

Compare and contrast essays

Explanatory compositions

Narrative Writing

Short fiction

Autobiographies

Responses to Literature

Writing in a log or journal

Writing short answers in a book guide

Persuasive Composition

Stating a position and supporting the position with evidence

Summary of Reading Materials

Writing the main idea

Writing a lab report

Taking notes on a textbook chapter

Research Report

Posing a question and providing support for the position taken, including documentation through footnotes, references, and/or a bibliography

One last thought...

Many writing exams are scored using a rubric. Ask for samples from your eighth grader's teacher, or find examples on the Internet. Rubrics are useful sources for seeing exactly what is expected.

More Than the Words

Editing, proofreading, and revising become increasingly important parts of the writing process this year. Conquer writer's block by using the following strategies to help improve your teen's writing skills.

Encourage *the following practices* to help improve your child's spelling and writing skills.

Spelling Notebook

Have your budding writer keep track of those difficult spelling words in a notebook. It saves time during the writing and revision stages.

Writer's Notebook

A writer's notebook can also include reminders of grammatical rules that are easy to break. For example, the apostrophe can show singular possession (the dog's bones) and plural possession (the dogs' bones). An apostrophe can substitute for removed letters in a contraction (*it's* for *it is*).

One last thought...

Your eighth grader may be using the computer for many projects. Keep in mind that spelling and grammar checkers help, but have to be monitored to be certain that the correction is correct. They aren't perfect!

Exploring
Vocabulary

The PSAT test, with its emphasis on vocabulary, is right around the corner. Your teen needs to learn more than definitions—how words relate or connect is equally important.

. . . .

Here are some other ideas for vocabulary development.

Analogies

Understanding member-group analogies, such as *fish is to school as student is to class,* is just one of several areas to explore.

SAT Vocabulary

Choose a word to incorporate into your conversation and challenge your teen to figure out what *your* word of the day is. In time, see if your teen can outsmart you!

Oxymoron

For more word fun, look for examples of *oxymorons*—a pair of words with contradictory meanings, such as *jumbo shrimp, near miss*, and *good grief.*

One last thought...

Improving vocabulary skills can also help improve your teen's reading comprehension!

Math

It's Not Always a Problem!

You may dread the notion of helping with math homework. Fortunately, you can find lots of help in your eighth grader's textbook, through resources the teacher can recommend, and by finding examples on the Internet.

Encourage the use of math with *these ideas.*

Be Creative

Math teachers say that approaching a problem with an open mind and thinking creatively help you come to a solution. This works especially well if the problem has multiple steps.

Day-to-Day Math

Model an interest in math and its utility, such as calculating your gas mileage or determining why your heating or water bills are so high. This will help build lifelong skills of money management.

Math Projects = Math Fun

Inventing, building and clothing design, making scale models—these all involve math. Most card and computer games are designed using statistics, probabilities, and algorithms. Challenge your teen to create a new game.

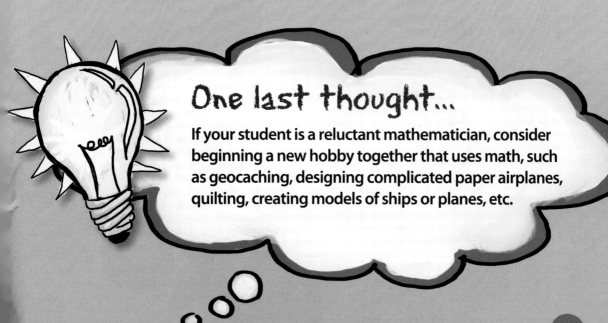

One last thought...

If your student is a reluctant mathematician, consider beginning a new hobby together that uses math, such as geocaching, designing complicated paper airplanes, quilting, creating models of ships or planes, etc.

FOIL
Method

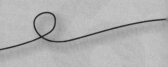

1. Use FOIL to multiply the terms inside the parentheses in a specific order: first, outside, inside, last.

$$(3X + 4)(X + 2)$$

2. **F**irst—multiply the first term in each set of parentheses.

$$(3X + 4)(X + 2) \longrightarrow 3X(X) = 3X^2$$

3. **O**utside—multiply the two terms on the outside.

$$(3X + 4)(X + 2) \longrightarrow 3X(2) = 6X$$

4. **I**nside—multiply both of the inside terms.

$$(3X + 4)(X + 2) \longrightarrow 4(X) = 4X$$

5. **L**ast—multiply the last term in each set of parentheses.

$$(3X + 4)(X + 2) \longrightarrow 4(2) = 8$$

6. Add everything together.

$$3X^2 + 6X + 4X + 8 \longrightarrow 3X^2 + 10X + 8$$

F O I L

Dive into Science

Eighth grade science includes an emphasis on the physical sciences, earth science, and the chemistry of life sciences. Memorization of terms and symbols also becomes increasingly important.

· ·

Use *these ideas* to help foster a greater understanding of science for your adolescent.

Science Classes

Keep your teen interested in science through university weekend classes or summer camps with a science or technology focus.

Science Programs

Check with local museums for science programs, or enlist the aid of a scientist friend who can help your teen learn about a topic of interest.

Online Help

If you aren't close to a university or a museum, check for online classes or check out www.sciencebuddies.org for more information.

One last thought...

There is a tremendous amount of vocabulary acquisition expected in a science class. Reinforce the words by playing some of the standard vocabulary games, such as concentration, word scrambles, and hangman.

Our Changing Country

Eighth graders will be focusing on U.S. history. From the founding days to the current challenges, students explore the significance of key periods, important leaders, and the contributions of other cultures.

Try some of these activities to foster interest in history.

Trip to the Past

Plan a trip into the past. Decide which period you'd want to visit and explore the food, dress, economy, politics, and pastimes.

Cuisines

Cook your way around the United States, starting with your region's foods.

Festivals

Attend local festivals that celebrate key events, that have reenactments, or that honor contributions to the United States from other cultures.

Virtual Museums

Visit websites of famous museums or landmarks of various cities and regions. In some museums, you can explore the museum without even stepping foot inside!

One last thought...

Delving into a major event, such as the Civil War, can build a lifelong interest in our history.

After-School
Action

Your teen needs a break in routine so that homework can be tackled. But the break should be productive as well.

Try some of these suggestions with your teen.

After-School Job

Soon your teen will be old enough to work in a public setting. This is the time to build some salable skills by offering services to trusted neighbors: yard jobs, snow removal, pet sitting, plant watering, etc.

Volunteer Work

Have your teen build community awareness skills by doing neighborhood volunteer work, such as babysitting, tutoring a younger student, or volunteering in a senior center.

Study Group

If your teen isn't part of an after-school club, have him or her join a study group at the library or school. Your teen might make some new friends!

Neighborhood Activities

Consider organizing your own neighborhood activity, taking turns with other parents to coach or supervise.

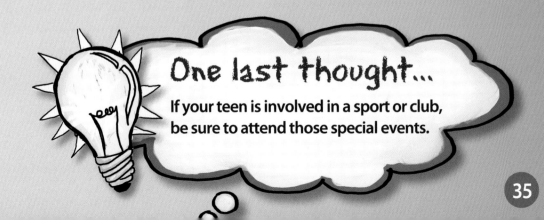

One last thought...

If your teen is involved in a sport or club, be sure to attend those special events.

Stay
Playful

Maintain fun with your teen *and* encourage him or her to make new friends. Social activity is very important at this age. Allow him or her to explore new friendships, but keep a close eye.

Consider trying some of these fun ideas with your teen.

Movie Time

Watch movies that interest your teen together.

Television Time

Keep the television in a central location, and join your teen in watching, even if you don't like the music or entertainers.

Sports

Learn a new sport or revisit a favorite. Invite your teen's friends along.

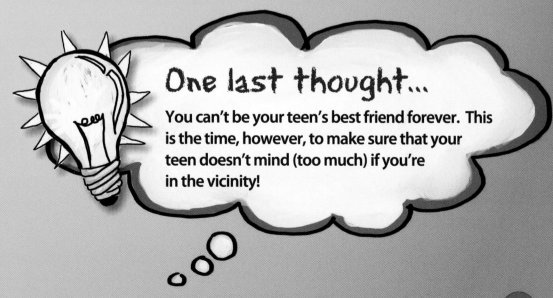

One last thought...

You can't be your teen's best friend forever. This is the time, however, to make sure that your teen doesn't mind (too much) if you're in the vicinity!

Trip
Tips

Reading a few "travel pages," even if they're limited to rediscovering your community or visiting cousins, is worth it. Have your teen help plan a real or virtual trip, from budgeting to finding various activities for the family to do.

Make it more productive
with some of these tips.

Speed Bump Ahead

Analyze the last trip—what worked? What didn't? Then, plan to make it better.

Itinerary

Have each family member plan an entire day or series of days: meal stops, entertainment, and the like. Record the schedule in advance so that there are no surprises.

Theme Trips

Choose a theme for the trip, such as finding the best water parks, burgers, wildlife, or ballparks.

Stay Active

Schedule time for a new or favorite activity.

Games

Have each family member be responsible for planning car games and rainy day board or card games.

Say Cheese

Invest in a digital camera and have your teen take on responsibility for documenting the trip and making a scrapbook.

One last thought...

Traveling is a great way to educate your child. It will be an invaluable experience that your child will never forget!

Dear Parent,

Abraham Lincoln once said, "The best thing about the future is that it comes one day at a time." This is good to remember during this busy year with your eighth grader. There are more challenges as you guide your teen past all those temptations and risks in the world. But your teen will be taking interesting classes and tackling all sorts of projects that will be fun to discuss. So enjoy that, too.

There are also great rewards in watching your teen move toward his or her future as a young adult. Enjoy the journey, and if you hit some speed bumps, remember that your teen's teachers and counselor stand ready to offer support. Have a great year!

Thank you!